WHAT DOES A TRUCK DRIVER DO?

F-92122

What Does a Community Helper Do?   Lisa Trumbauer

Words to Know

cargo (CAR-goh)—Goods, or things, carried on trucks, trains, ships, and airplanes.

CB radio (see-bee RAY-dee-oh)—A kind of two-way radio that lets truck drivers talk to each other.

deliver (duh-LIV-ur)—To bring goods from one place to another.

route (root)—A regular road, path, or way of traveling.

weigh station (way STAY-shun)—An area set up on the side of some highways to weigh trucks. The station makes sure trucks are safe and not too heavy.

Enslow Elementary

an imprint of

Enslow Publishers, Inc.

40 Industrial Road PO Box 38
Box 398 Aldershot
Berkeley Heights, NJ 07922 Hants GU12 6BP
USA UK

http://www.enslow.com

Contents

Truck drivers make sure their **cargo** arrives safely in their big trucks.

Moving Day!

Today is moving day. A big truck pulls up to our house. The driver climbs down from the cab. The truck driver will move our things from our old house to our new house.

The inside of a truck has many switches, buttons, and dials. Truck drivers must learn how to work all of them.

Driving Safely

Trucks are hard to drive. Truck drivers must learn how to safely drive them. They go to school to learn to drive a truck.

This truck driver checks the truck's oil.

cab

trailer

Truck drivers check their trucks. They make sure the trucks are safe. They connect the big trailer to the cab. They check the air in the tires. Some trucks have eighteen tires in all! Truck drivers also check the oil in the engine.

This truck driver is loading a big machine onto his truck.

These truck drivers are loading boxes to take to a family's new home.

On the Road

Truck drivers read maps. They plan the route that they will drive. They learn all the highways and roads. Truck drivers deliver cargo, like food, clothes, and furniture. They take their cargo to towns all over the country.

A **CB radio** lets truck drivers talk to each other while on the road.

Truck drivers talk on CB radios. They talk to other truck drivers. The drivers tell each other about problems on the road.

Truck drivers can rest and get gas for their trucks at truck stops.

Resting and Sleeping

Truck drivers need to rest. They need to sleep, eat, and stretch their legs. Truck stops are places right off the highway. Here truck drivers eat and talk to friends. They also check their trucks and get gas.

Truck drivers sometimes drive long hours. They can sleep right in the cab of their trucks.

After a rest, they go on the road again. Truck drivers may drive all day. They see many places. Sometimes they drive at night, too. When they get sleepy, they may sleep in the cab.

This truck slows down and waits its turn at the **weigh station**.

Is the Truck Too Heavy?

Truck drivers stop at weigh stations. The truck sits on a big scale. The scale shows if the truck is too heavy. If a truck is too heavy, it might not be safe to drive. These stations make sure the truck is safe.

The truck has arrived safely.

This family is glad the truck driver brought their things.

The Truck Is Here!

The moving truck is here! It has been a long trip. The truck driver safely delivered all our things. I wonder where the truck driver will go next?

Moving Day Map

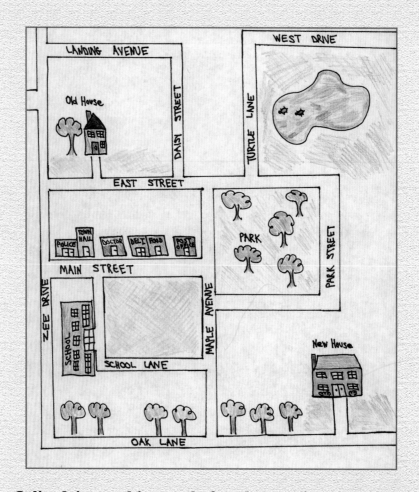

Julie drives a big truck for the moving company. She is helping the Williams family move across town. Help Julie find her way from the old house to the new house. Can you find the shortest way? How about the longest way? Can you write the directions for the shortest and longest route?

Learn More

Books

Gibson, Karen Bush. *Community Helpers: Truck Drivers*. Mankato, MN: Bridgestone Books, 2001.

Liebman, Dan. *I Want to Be a Truck Driver*. Richmond Hill, Ontario: Firefly Books, 2001.

Mitchell, Joyce Stayton. *Tractor-Trailer Trucker: A Powerful Truck Book*. Berkeley, Calif.: Tricycle Press, 2000.

Internet Addresses

Kids' Quiz to Learn About Trucking
<http://www.thetruckersreport.com/KidsCorner/kids_quiz_to_learn_about_truckin.shtml>
Take this quiz to help you learn about trucking.

Maps Home Page
<http://academic.brooklyn.cuny.edu/geology/leveson/core/linksa/maptop.html>
Learn about maps.

Index

Note to Teachers and Parents: The *What Does a Community Helper Do?* series supports curriculum standards for K–4 learning about community services and helpers. The Words to Know section introduces subject-specific vocabulary. Early readers may require help with these new words.

Series Literacy Consultant:
Allan A. De Fina, Ph.D.
Past President of the New Jersey Reading Association
Professor, Department of Literacy Education
New Jersey City University

Enslow Elementary, an imprint of Enslow Publishers, Inc.

Enslow Elementary® is a registered trademark
of Enslow Publishers, Inc.

Copyright © 2006 by Enslow Publishers, Inc.

Library of Congress Cataloging-in-Publication Data

Trumbauer, Lisa, 1963–
    What does a truck driver do? / Lisa Trumbauer.
        p. cm. — (What does a community helper do?)
    Includes bibliographical references and index.
    ISBN 0-7660-2324-9
    1. Truck drivers—Vocational guidance—Juvenile
    literature. I. Title. II. Series.
    HD8039.M795T78 2005
    388.3'24'023—dc22   2005009785

Printed in the United States of America

10 9 8 7 6 5 4 3 2 1

To Our Readers:
We have done our best to make sure all Internet Addresses in this book were active and appropriate when we went to press. However, the author and the publisher have no control over and assume no liability for the material available on those Internet sites or on other Web sites they may link to. Any comments or suggestions can be sent by e-mail to comments@enslow.com or to the address on the back cover.

Illustration Credits: brand X pictures, pp. 4 (top and bottom), 10 (bottom), 20 (top and bottom); comstock.com, pp. 1, 6 (top and bottom), 8, 10 (top), 12, 14 (top and bottom), 16 (top), 18; Enslow Publishers, Inc., p. 22; Hemera Technologies, Inc. 1997–2000, pp. 2, 9, 13, 17; Reality, p. 16 (bottom).

Cover Illustration: comstock.com (bottom); top left to right (comstock.com, first three photos; brand X pictures, fourth photo).